Respecting Others

by Robin Nelson

first step nonfiction

Lerner Publications Company · Minneapolis

I can decide how to act.

I try to act with **respect.**

I respect myself.

I eat foods that are good
for me.

I respect my friends.

I play **fair.**

I respect my parents.

I do my **chores.**

I respect my teacher.

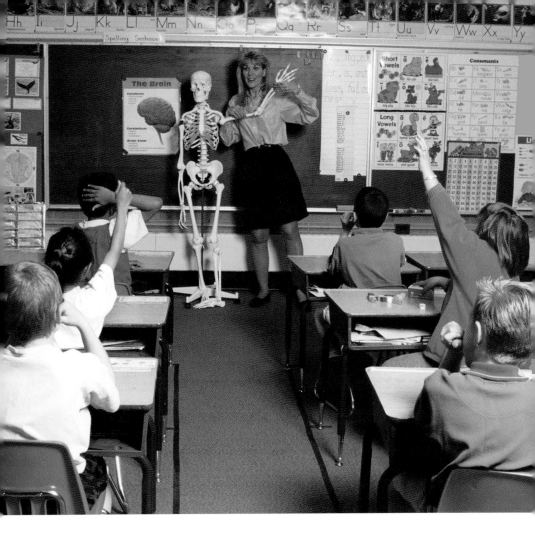

I listen carefully.

I respect people I don't know.

I have good **manners.**

I respect the earth.

I do not litter.

I think about what I do.

Everyone **deserves** respect.

How can you respect others at home?

- Listen to your brother's or sister's ideas.

- Give everyone in your family privacy.

- Say "please" and "thank you."

- Share your toys.

- Don't take things without asking.

How can you respect others at school?

- Don't talk when others are talking.

- Listen to other people's ideas.

- Don't judge someone by the way they look.

- Give everyone a chance to play.

- Pay attention to your teacher.

Glossary

 chores – tasks that need to be done

 deserves – has the right to; is worthy of

 fair – treating everyone the same

 manners – behaviors

 respect – honor

Index

The photographs in this book are reproduced through the courtesy of: © PhotoDisc, front cover, pp. 6, 11, 14; © Rubberball Productions, pp. 2, 3, 22 (bottom); © Corbis Royalty Free, pp. 4, 16; Brand-X Pictures, pp. 5, 8, 17, 22 (second from top); © H. Rogers/TRIP, pp. 7, 22 (middle); © Fotografia, Inc./CORBIS, pp. 9, 22 (top); © Tom McCarthy/TRANSPARENCIES, Inc., p. 10; © J. Faircloth/TRANSPARENCIES, Inc., p. 12; © Norvia Behling, pp. 13, 22 (second from bottom); © Connie Summers, p. 15.

Illustrations on page 19 and 21 by Tim Seeley.

Library binding by Lerner Publications Company
A division of Lerner Publishing Group
241 First Avenue North
Minneapolis, MN 55401 USA

Website address: www.lernerbooks.com

Library of Congress Cataloging-in-Publication Data

Nelson, Robin, 1971–
    Respecting others / by Robin Nelson.
      p.   cm. — (First step nonfiction)
    Includes index.
    Summary: An introduction to respecting yourself, friends, parents, teachers, people you don't know, and the earth, with specific examples of how to show respect at home and at school.
    ISBN: 0–8225–1286–6 (lib. bdg. : alk. paper)
    1. Respect for persons—Juvenile literature. 2. Respect—Juvenile literature. 3. Children—Conduct of life—Juvenile literature. [1. Respect. 2. Conduct of life.] I. Title. II. Series.
BJ1533.R42 N45 2003
179'.9—dc21
2002000594

Manufactured in the United States of America
3 4 5 6 7 8 – DP – 09 08 07 06 05 04